HOW TO
Reset

SIMPLE TIPS TO HELP YOU REDISCOVER
YOURSELF AND LIVE LIFE TO THE FULL

VICKI VRINT

HOW TO RESET

An Hachette UK Company
www.hachette.co.uk

Vie Books, an imprint of Summersdale Publishers Ltd
Part of Octopus Publishing Group Limited
Carmelite House
50 Victoria Embankment
LONDON
EC4Y 0DZ
UK

Printed and bound in China

ISBN: 978-1-80007-167-4

Substantial discounts on bulk quantities of Summersdale books are available to corporations, professional associations and other organizations. For details contact general enquiries: telephone: +44 (0) 1243 771107 or email: enquiries@summersdale.com.

Contents

Introduction...6

Part One:
Where am I now?.......................................8

Part Two:
What matters to me?...............................36

Part Three:
Where do I want to be?...........................68

Part Four:
How will I get there?..............................86

Part Five:
What does my support system look like?............................128

Conclusion...156

INTRODUCTION

Most of us are so busy living our lives that we rarely get the chance to stand back and reflect on how things are going. We don't pause to take stock, weigh up our choices and fix the things that niggle us, whether it's because we don't have time or we're simply not in the habit.

However, the benefits of a little time out – time to reset – are huge. We can remind ourselves of the important things in life, the things that matter most to us, and prioritize them. We can also think about what's not working and deal with those areas too. Resetting means taking back control of your life and rebalancing it. It's about being able to make time for the things you love, which bring you joy and fulfilment, and steering away from any negatives that bring you down. Recognizing both these things can take time and practice, and knowing where to start can be even more challenging – which is where this book comes in.

These pages will show you, step by step, how to clear the decks and move on to a happier and healthier future. It will inspire you, prompt you and guide you toward making a fresh start, whether that involves making a few tweaks or tackling a challenging area that needs a little more work. Difficult past events can have lasting effects that put a negative spin on the way we live day to day, but here you'll learn how to turn these tough experiences into positives and find ways to move forward in a meaningful way.

So welcome to your gentle journey of recovery and rediscovery, a chance to reset and rebalance your life.

Part One:

WHERE AM I NOW?

The first step in your journey to resetting your life and rediscovering yourself is to take stock of where you are now. This chapter will help you consider the different areas of your life and decide what is – and what isn't – currently working for you. It will help you to reflect on your health, mental well-being, relationships and career. We'll also discover some new ways to press pause and reflect, to look at how you currently spend your time and to get together a pretty impressive list of your skills and achievements. A perfect place to start!

Taking time to think

To reset your life, you'll need to take time out to reflect. A perfect solution would be taking some time off work, away from your regular commitments, to give yourself a chance to relax and get some perspective on things. If this is an option for you, it's a brilliant way to start your reset mission: booking a weekend away somewhere peaceful to spend time connecting with nature and working through the exercises in this book would be ideal.

Don't worry if you can't plan a trip; you can still make regular time to pause, check in with yourself and focus on what's important to you. Start your reset journey by setting aside some time each week to reflect. You might find 15 minutes to yourself during your lunch break or evening, or decide that a quiet hour alone on a Sunday morning will work for you.

If you're brave enough to say goodbye, life will reward you with a new hello.

Paulo Coelho

THE IMPORTANCE OF SELF-CARE

Whether you're on a mission to reboot your life or not, it's essential to regularly "press pause" and give your mind a chance to process everything you've experienced. If you don't do this your sleep and mood will suffer, so make a vow to take some time to yourself every day, even if all you do is sit quietly and breathe.

If finding daily downtime is genuinely impossible, turn to page 90 for tips on claiming back some of your day. In the meantime, try to fit in mini self-care hits. Take 5 minutes on your break to chat with a friend or read an inspiring article, or listen to a favourite track while you're waiting for the kettle to boil. Stepping outside to get some fresh air is another great option.

Breathing reset

Wherever you are and whatever you're doing, learning to focus on your breathing will give you the chance to reset your emotions and ground yourself. This breathing exercise is an easy way to improve your breathing technique and a great mindfulness exercise too.

Ideally, we should breathe slowly and deeply, but most of us snatch speedy breaths and miss out on the clarity and energy that breathing in enough oxygen gives us. Try this exercise at the start of any self-care session or whenever you need to calm down or re-energize during the day.

Simply breathe in through your nose for a slow count of four, feeling your lungs inflate and your chest rise. Hold your breath for a count of two and then exhale through your mouth for a count of six. (The longer out-breath sends a signal to your brain that turns down your stress response, so this is very calming.)

A space to reflect

It's a nice idea to create a cosy space for self-reflection, even if it's just a favourite armchair or a beanbag in the corner of your bedroom. Add a few creature comforts if you can – cushions, an inspirational picture, candles or a lamp. A view of the outside world is very calming, and if you're lucky enough to live somewhere warm and can take your self-care outside, that's even better. A picnic blanket under a tree or a seat in your favourite corner of the park will give you the benefits of daylight and fresh air while you reflect.

You might like to make a ritual of entering your reflection space. You could turn off your phone and any other distractions, for example, and settle down with a hot drink. Then take a few calming breaths and you're ready to begin.

EVERY DAY
IS A NEW PAGE
OF YOUR STORY
WAITING TO
BE WRITTEN.

STARTING YOUR JOURNEY

It's a good idea to start a journal to record your thoughts as you work through this book. Journaling is a wonderfully calming activity, and there's no pressure to do it every day. Your journal is a trusted friend – it's there waiting for you whenever you need to offload your thoughts, and it will hold your memories until you need to dip into them again.

Your journal is also a great place to try free-writing, a practice that helps you unlock your feelings. To start, simply sit down and write whatever comes into your head – without stopping to edit your words – for as long as feels comfortable. It's a great way to relax into any of the exercises in this book, and reading your words back can be quite revealing.

Let's use a free-writing exercise to help you think about where you are in your life right now. You're going to introduce yourself to your journal. Turn to a new page and write the words: "Hello, my name is [insert your name here] and I'm…" Then continue writing, noting down whatever first comes to mind. Aim to write a page or so. Give this a go now, before reading on.

How did you get on? Take a look back at what you wrote. How did you define yourself – did you talk about your career, your emotions or your role in your family? (Any themes that stand out will, of course, reveal what's important to you.) And how did you complete that opening sentence? Whether it was "I'm tired", "I'm a student", "I'm lost" or even "I'm hungry", this can give you a pointer toward any areas you'd like to prioritize.

Now your brain has "warmed up", have a think about the areas of your life that are bringing you joy and note these down. And are there any areas that aren't going so well? How would you like to improve these? It may be that you're generally happy but are looking for a new challenge, or perhaps you feel pretty negative about an issue or two. Whatever the case, you've already taken a step in the right direction by thinking through what matters to you, and so you're one step closer to devising a plan to move forward. The next step is looking at your current situation in a little more detail.

We do not learn
from experience,
we learn from
reflecting on
experience.

John Dewey

Mood trackers

Mood trackers help you to see the bigger picture in terms of how you're feeling, helping you spot patterns in your mood and identify what triggers these feelings. For instance, you might see that you always have a low mood the evening before you're due to return to work or a high mood after your weekly walk in the woods. A mood tracker helps you to realize what an impact these activities have on your happiness levels.

There are plenty of mood-tracking apps out there, but it's very satisfying to fill in a paper-based tracker. The simplest involve completing a square per day with an emoji or colour to represent how you're feeling. You can record more entries per day if you like (for morning, afternoon and evening), or get really creative and draw something more elaborate – a flower with a petal for every day of the month, for example. Try completing yours every evening to see what it reveals.

HOW ARE YOU FEELING?

How are you doing? It's a question we ask others every day, but few of us ask this of ourselves. Carrying out a well-being audit to get a clear picture of how you're feeling will help you identify areas to prioritize – and it will also be something to look back on later down the line, to see the positive changes that self-care can bring.

There are some excellent online questionnaires that assess your mental well-being; obviously, it's important to use one from a reputable source. The NHS website offers a mood assessment quiz which has been designed by mental-health professionals to help you reflect on your mood over the past couple of weeks. It identifies your levels of anxiety and depression, and offers practical tips on coping with any issues that come up. The Oxford Happiness Questionnaire will help you assess your levels of happiness and enjoyment, while Mental Health America offers a range of online tests to assess you for different mental well-being issues. (For under 16s, visit the Young Minds website.)

If you do find that you're experiencing anxiety or depression, try not to be too hard on yourself. One in four of us will experience mental-health issues at some point in our lives, and these are usually an effect of challenging situations we've faced. It is nothing to be ashamed of, and there is plenty you can do to improve things. In the short term, you can lift your mood and decrease your stress levels by:

- connecting with others – phone or visit a friend

- getting active – go for a walk, run or have a dance around the living room

- paying attention to the present moment – savour a coffee, focus on the details of a favourite photo

- including some time to indulge yourself every day

If you're struggling or your mood is having an impact on your day-to-day life, chat to your healthcare professional who will be able to advise you on the support available to you. Charities such as Mind and Mental Health America have plenty of information online too.

At the moment my mood is:

....
....

My low points happen when:

....
....

I can improve things by:

....
....

A HEALTH AND FITNESS CHECK

Let's get physical and think about your fitness. First of all, take a look at the following questions and note down some thoughts in your journal or below.

How do you feel about exercise?   ☺   😐   ☹

Why?

....

How often do you exercise?

....

What type of exercise do you enjoy?

....

What type of exercise would you like to try?

....

How would you describe your fitness levels overall?
How is your stamina?

1   2   3   4   5   6   7   8   9   10

How is your flexibility?

1   2   3   4   5   6   7   8   9   10

How is your strength?

1   2   3   4   5   6   7   8   9   10

How is your energy level?

1   2   3   4   5   6   7   8   9   10

What would you like to improve?

....

Use these questions to help you identify areas to improve. You may already have a fitness regime that you enjoy, but it can be fun to think of other activities you might like to try, and to set yourself some goals. We'll look at ways to improve fitness on page 60.

You can carry out a more detailed fitness assessment with the help of a stopwatch and a tape measure. The Mayo Clinic website includes a series of self-tests to help you measure your heart rate, aerobic fitness (jogging test), strength (push-up test or sit-up test) and flexibility (sit-and-reach test). They're good fun to do, and if you keep a note of your results now you'll be able to look back and see any improvements. If you'd rather not pit yourself against the "average" results listed online, simply count how many sit-ups, push-ups, squats and star jumps you can do in 30-second bursts and keep a note of them.

It's also worth thinking about whether you have any health issues or concerns that you need to sort out. Perhaps you've been putting off a dental check or a health screening, or have some symptoms that you've been meaning to get checked out. Bite the bullet and get some advice or book an appointment today. You'll feel much better for taking action.

HOW'S YOUR JOB WORKING OUT?

Wherever you work and whatever you do, it's important that you get some satisfaction from your job. You might not love every aspect of it, but you should certainly feel that the pros outweigh the cons and that you can find purpose in your work, whether that's progressing up the career ladder, or simply getting on with your colleagues and collecting your pay cheque at the end of the month.

In an ideal world, your job would give you all the positives: progression, pride, recognition for your efforts and a decent rate of pay. Of course, for many of us our work won't tick every one of these boxes, but if you regularly feel unhappy about going in to work or you don't get on with your colleagues, it's time to rethink and reset your working life. Over the next couple of chapters you'll get the chance to explore the things that really matter to you, and consider whether a change of direction would suit you, but in the meantime use these prompts to help you assess how you feel right now about your current role.

How do you feel about your job?

What do you like about it?

....

And what don't you like?

....

Do you feel as though you're making a difference at work?

Yes/No

Do you get positive feedback for your efforts?

Yes/No

Do you like your co-workers?

Yes/No

Are you proud of your contribution?

Yes/No

Do you have some freedom to make decisions in your job?

Yes/No

What would you like to change?

....

EVERY CHOICE
IS A CHANCE
TO CHANGE.

CELEBRATE YOUR SPECIAL SKILLS

Most of us tend to focus on our "fails" rather than our achievements, so it's a good idea to get together a list of all your "wins", a confidence-boosting record of all the things you're proud of. Take a page in your journal and list everything from your junior school swimming certificate onward! You could start a file of mementoes and photos to remind you of your successes. Ask your family or friends for ideas about what to include too.

And remember, it's not all about exams and certificates; you may have achieved the impossible and got through a whole day without your kids arguing, or managed to make your grumpy neighbour smile – they're all achievements too. For everything you write down, make a note of the skills you used to make it happen and then take a page to summarize these. Read this through regularly to remind yourself that you're brilliant and to reset your confidence levels.

REVIEW YOUR RELATIONSHIPS

Maintaining strong positive relationships is essential for our mental well-being, but when life gets hectic, we tend to prioritize work and other commitments over our private lives. Our loved ones will always be there for us, but it's important to make time to enjoy those relationships and maintain them too. Just as positive interactions have an uplifting effect on us, negative ones can be draining and toxic, so have a relationship review to consider how you can improve your connections.

List your family, friends and colleagues and think through each relationship in turn. Is it uplifting? What's working well? Do you have any issues? Do you feel energized or drained after seeing that person? Once you've got a clear picture of the relationship, think about what you'd like to change. Could you strengthen your connection by phoning once a week, clearing the air after an argument or trying a new and exciting activity together? Make sure you haven't fallen into the trap of regularly offloading all your problems onto a friend without giving them a chance to chat too. Positive relationships should be a two-way street.

For relationships that aren't so positive, consider how you could improve them or even minimize your contact with the person involved. You shouldn't feel drained, judged or downtrodden when you're with others. It's fine to turn down invitations that would involve you enduring the company of people who aren't your tribe. If you're working with difficult people, try having a conversation to clear the air or simply move on – toxic folk bring you down.

If you're in a couple, this relationship will probably be one of the most important in your life, but it can be one of the most neglected. Small gestures can make a big difference, though, so think about ways to show your appreciation for your other half – carrying out a random act of kindness every day, for example – and set aside time alone together. If you have bigger issues to address, take a look at page 120 for ideas on resetting your relationship. Some couples find that a regular relationship review works for them – a chance to chat through any problems that crop up. If this appeals, try to be tactful and diplomatic about any issues you raise, and remember it's best avoided if either of you is tired or in a bad mood!

Step out of the
history that is
holding you back.
Step into the new
story you are
willing to create.

Oprah Winfrey

LEAVE THE
PAST BEHIND,
BUT CARRY
YOUR EXPERIENCE
FORWARD.

HOW DO YOU SPEND YOUR TIME?

The last area we need to take stock of is your time and the way that you spend it. It's tricky to get a clear picture of this when you're rushing from one commitment to the next, so the best way to do it is to chart your activities over the next couple of weeks. Draw out a chart for the week with a column for each day and times marked down the sides (see page 33), then fill in how you spend the day, trying to give as accurate an idea of the time spent as you can – without getting out your stopwatch! You can also add an emoji or note at the bottom of each column to show whether the day was a mad rush or felt balanced.

Look through your chart at the end of the week to see whether there are any surprises. Mark any time you had to yourself to pursue your own interests or relax, and mark any really challenging or difficult periods that left you feeling stressed. We're going to look at how to reduce the stressful moments and increase your "you time" in Part Four – by the end of your reset journey, you'll have reclaimed control over how you spend your days.

	MONDAY	TUESDAY	WEDNESDAY	THURSDAY	FRIDAY	SATURDAY	SUNDAY
MORNING							
LUNCHTIME							
AFTERNOON							
EVENING							
NOTES							

Where you're at

Well done for completing this first chapter and taking a look at how things stand now. Use this page to summarize where you've got to.

Generally I feel:

....

I would like to feel more:

....

Things that are working well:

....

Things I would like to change:

....

My special skills are:

....

My good friends are:

....

What I would like to achieve by resetting my life:

....

All done? Brilliant! Remember, don't feel downhearted if your review has highlighted a few problem areas – this is just your starting point and every step you take as you work through this book will be toward a more positive and rewarding future. So let's take the next step now and work out what matters to you most.

Start where you are.
Use what you have.
Do what you can.

Arthur Ashe

Part Two:

WHAT MATTERS TO ME?

If you ask yourself what matters to you in life, chances are you'll be able to pick out a few easy answers, such as friends, family and chocolate! But think a little more deeply and you can work out your core values – the ideas and principles that really resonate with you – and identifying these will help you to live a much more fulfilling life. When you know what matters to you, you can make decisions more easily, prioritize your activities and set goals that fit with your moral code.

Don't worry if this sounds complicated; this chapter includes plenty of prompts and practical ideas to help you work out what makes you tick, as well as ways to identify your favourite activities and social priorities too. Seeing yourself anew is a powerful and positive part of the reset process, so turn the page and get ready to get to know yourself a little better.

This is me!

Creative projects are beneficial on so many levels. As mindful activities, they help us to relax and reside in the moment, but they can also create a state of "flow", where your brain is completely focused on the task in hand – you're relaxed, absorbed and your ego is disengaged. Flow activities are a perfect gateway to discovering your *self*, so creating something that represents you as a person can be rewarding and very revealing.

Pick a craft that you enjoy and create a piece titled "This is me!". You could paint a picture or draw a cartoon, write a poem or story; sum yourself up in a playlist or Pinterest board; film your own biopic; make a collage; sew a quilt; design a flow chart... However you express yourself, enjoy creating your artwork, then reflect on your finished piece and the elements you chose to represent you.

WHAT DO YOU LOVE TO DO?

It's so important to do the things that make us happy: for our mental and physical health, to combat anxiety and stress... and, of course, because it's fun! But if your days have become filled with tasks that are definitely not your favourite pastimes, you might find it tricky to even remember the things you enjoy doing, let alone fit them in. We'll look at some smart ways to reorganize your time on page 90 but for now, take a moment to remind yourself of the things you love doing – activities that bring you joy and give your day a boost.

Take a page in your journal, or use the prompts on the following page, to note down the activities you need in your life to make you happy, the things that make you feel most fulfilled. It might be a weekly walk through the park, your martial arts class, or the evening you spend catching up with friends or studying a new skill. (We often lose track of time when we're carrying out these joyful activities and an hour can speed by in what feels like minutes.)

If you're stuck for ideas, look back on your week and think about the high points – or make a note of your happy moments in the week ahead. What were you doing when you felt happy? You could also try flicking through your photos or online posts to jog your memory, or even thinking back to the activities you enjoyed as a child.

Looking for themes in your happy moments will help you identify what's important to you – it might be exercise, family time, a connection with nature, relaxation, a sense of achievement – and this makes it easier to consider how you can fit more of this into your week. You may even be able to think of new activities to try that would bring you this happiness.

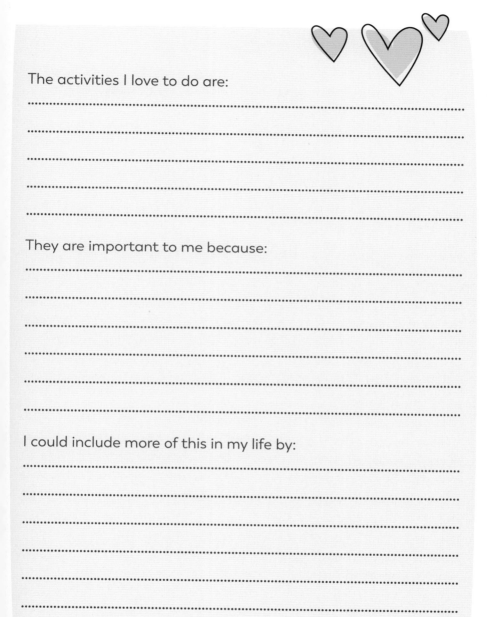

The activities I love to do are:

....

....

....

....

....

They are important to me because:

....

....

....

....

....

....

I could include more of this in my life by:

....

....

....

....

....

....

KEEP A GRATITUDE JOURNAL

Considering the things you're grateful for is another way to identify what matters to you. Reflect on your day as you drop off to sleep and pick out the moment(s) that brought you joy, no matter how small. Focusing on these will mean you end the day on a positive note. The more you practise, the more positives you'll find, and you'll appreciate these moments in the future more greatly too.

Keep track of these moments in your journal, use a gratitude app or create a folder of photos on your phone. This will make it easy to spot the things that matter most to you. If the majority of your special moments are the ones you spend with your friends, or you have a folder full of pictures from your walks in the countryside, it's easy to see that those are the things you value most – and the things you can prioritize in your new, reset life.

When I started
counting my
blessings, my whole
life turned around.

Willie Nelson

The people you admire

An easy way to identify the qualities that matter to you is to think about the people you most admire. Make a list of five (or more!) people you've always looked up to – this could include your childhood heroes, inspirational celebrities or family members or friends that have had a big influence on you. Once you've got your list, note down the reasons these people inspire you. You're likely to discover that many of them share a quality that you value highly, whether that's their authenticity, their bravery or their unique sense of humour. Record that quality below so you can come back to it whenever you need:

The quality that I most admire in others is:

....

....

Acknowledging the qualities that matter to us can help us to value and curate our friendships. It also allows us to set our own self-development goals, as we will know which aspects we'd like to include more of in our lives ahead.

LET YOUR
FRIENDS INSPIRE
YOU; THEY'RE
EVERYDAY
HEROES.

YOUR CORE VALUES

Once you've identified the quality you value most in others, you will find it easier to put together a list of your own core values – the principles you would like to live your life by. Which values are most important to you? Circle the ones that stand out to you on the list below, or jot down your own ideas in your journal.

Honesty	Appreciation	Enthusiasm
Loyalty	Positivity	Compassion
Kindness	Authenticity	Confidence
Courage	Intelligence	Acceptance
Balance	Encouragement	Clear-thinking

Now see if you can prioritize your principles and list your top three:

My top three core values are:

....

....

....

Consider ways you can practise these in your day-to-day life. You may like to write them down and pin them somewhere prominent to inspire you, or you could make them into a mantra to repeat every morning – "I am compassionate, courageous and authentic", for example.

These principles will make an excellent guide for you, moving forward. Whenever you find yourself in a difficult situation, pause and take a breath before reminding yourself of your core values. If you act in a way that honours them, you will be making a considered and authentic decision.

FIND YOUR MOTIVATION

You've thought about the qualities you admire and the activities you enjoy, but there's one more area to explore in your quest to work out what makes you tick – your motivation. Why do you do the things you do? Finding your "why" will help you understand what's missing from any areas of your life that aren't so satisfying at the moment, and it will enable you to set some exciting new goals too.

Look back and remind yourself of the moments that were the most satisfying, the times when you felt the most accomplished and enthusiastic about what you were doing. Were there particular tasks you enjoyed more than others? Did you get a feeling of achievement when you carried out an act of kindness or negotiated an agreement between friends who had fallen out? Or did you feel most inspired when you were doing something creative or learning a new skill?

List these moments in your journal and look for the "why" behind them. (We tend to be most motivated by things that matter to us and activities that we're good at.) What made these moments so satisfying? Were you teaching, learning, nurturing, mediating, organizing, supporting, helping or creating? Which of these motivates you most? This is your why.

I feel most motivated when I'm:

....

....

....

....

Now think about your job, home life or studies and consider how often you get the chance to carry out tasks that fit with your "why". If you feel highly motivated when you're creating things, for example, do you get the chance to use your creative skills in your day job? If not, your work is not in line with your sense of purpose, and you're likely to feel uninspired and demotivated. Are there ways you could tweak your job to make it more satisfying, or could you take on a creative project outside of work to inspire and enthuse you while you think about other options?

How you spend
your energy is
ultimately what
creates who you are.

Susan Sarandon

Review your time

Once you've identified the things that matter to you it can be useful to look again at the way you spend your time and see just how often you get a chance to experience these things in your week. Look back at your chart that shows how you spent your time and shade in the moments where you were doing things that made you happy, spending time with the people that matter or pursuing your purpose. Did these things crop up regularly?

You may just need to tweak your schedule a little to improve things – to include some time to study or play sport every week, for example, or to fit in some quality time with a loved one – but if you currently have very few purposeful or positive experiences in your week, it's time to make some bigger changes to bring your life in line with your priorities.

WHAT DOESN'T MATTER?

You've worked out the important things in your life; now it's time to take a good hard look at the other things you give your energy to and decide whether they deserve a place in your routine. Obviously, everyone has certain chores and responsibilities that they need to carry out – such as housework and caring for others – but consider the other activities you fit into your week. Why are you doing them? Are they tasks that you carry out because you feel you ought to? Are there activities that you dislike or that drain you?

Many of us take on extra responsibilities because we feel it's expected of us, or because we want to gain approval from others. If we do this too often, we can end up living a life that doesn't fit with our own priorities, and this will never feel satisfying. Reassess your commitments and remind yourself that it is okay to say a polite no to the things that you would rather not do. "I'm sorry I can't help out this time" is a good way to do this – there's no need to offer any excuse or explanation. It may feel tricky at first, but stay strong and remember that your reward will be more time to devote to the activities and causes that really matter to you.

Just as decluttering your schedule will clear the decks for a calmer and more purposeful life, decluttering your surroundings will free up your energy and time too. It's so easy to fill our homes with "stuff" that we don't use and to hang on to things that we no longer need, but being surrounded by unwanted belongings is draining and depressing. It's impossible to underestimate the positive power of having a good sort-out – and it's amazing what you can achieve in 10 minutes a day of decluttering.

Start small – perhaps with a single drawer or a cupboard – and clear the items in that area, thinking about whether you really need them. Clean the area you've cleared, then only put back the things you want to keep, donating the rest to charity or another good home. It's a good idea to dispose of old paperwork, piles of leaflets and unwanted gifts too – we all tend to hang on to these for longer than we need. You'll get such a boost as you see the results of your efforts and may feel inspired to make a fresh start.

Make it a mission

A fun way to help you consolidate everything you've thought about so far is to write a mission statement to tell the world what you're about. You can make this as serious or humorous as you like; the main thing is to get all your priorities together in one place. You might say:

I'm Nadeem and I stand for authenticity. I value my friends for their honesty and courage and am striving to bring these qualities to my day-to-day life. I'm an expert organizer and am rightly proud of my super-organized sock drawer. I recently rediscovered my love of making music and play guitar every week.

I'm Elizabeth, I'm 32 and I represent working mums everywhere. I love learning, caring for others... and watching Netflix. I'm passionate about wildlife and have just started volunteering at my local animal shelter. I commit to learning from my mistakes, embracing the chaos and prioritizing the people I love.

INCLUDE THE ESSENTIALS

There are certain things that we all need in our lives to enjoy positive mental health. It's likely that you've identified some of these already while working through this chapter, but just to be absolutely sure, here's a reminder of the essentials. If these activities don't matter to you yet, they should! Now that you've decluttered your schedule, you can add in these essentials to reset your life on a happier and healthier path.

Six essentials for a positive life:

1. Time spent outdoors, connecting with nature.

2. Exercise.

3. A healthy diet and plenty of water.

4. Interaction with others.

5. A sense of purpose.

6. Time to meditate or reflect.

MARVEL AT THE WONDERS OF NATURE

AND REMEMBER THAT YOU'RE ONE OF THEM.

RESET YOUR RELATIONSHIP WITH NATURE

The mood-boosting benefits of time spent outdoors are well known, so it's important to get outside regularly. Long weekend walks in the countryside are wonderful for your body and mind, but getting outside for a short time every day helps you to build a real bond with nature, which is even more beneficial. Whether you live in the country or the city, the great outdoors is never far away if you look hard enough. If your relationship with wildlife has lapsed, here are some simple ways to get your nature fix and reset your connection with the natural world.

1. **Invite nature into your home, garden or outside space:** you could plant wildflowers, grow herbs in a window box, make a bee hotel, hang up bird feeders or fix them to your windows, or create a woodpile for invertebrates.

2. **Look for your nearest wild patch:** visit it regularly, noting how it changes through the seasons.

3. **Research your favourite animal, tree or plant:** look up some fascinating facts about it or investigate its role in evolution or myth. Meditate on its qualities, spot it in the wild, or draw, paint or celebrate it in any way you choose.

4. **Include a walk or quick break outside as part of your daily routine:** pair it up with something you already do regularly (taking out the rubbish, your trip to work, going to the shop for milk, etc.). Look for birds, flowers and trees along your route and appreciate their details.

5. **Get active outdoors:** set yourself a challenge of either walking, running, cycling or swimming somewhere wild and beautiful.

6. **Support nature in your area:** you could volunteer to do a beach clean, set up a wildlife corner, help at an animal rescue centre or join a conservation group at your local nature reserve.

7. **Compile an album of photos with a natural theme:** you could be inspired by cloudscapes, leaves or birds sitting on street furniture.

ENJOY EXERCISE

Regular exercise is essential for maintaining our physical fitness, avoiding disease and boosting our mental well-being. If you're less than enthusiastic about exercise at the moment, now's the time to tune in to its benefits and plan an inspirational fitness regime that suits you.

Which of the benefits of exercise is most important to you? Is it improved fitness, increased energy or a feeling of achievement as you master a new skill? Would you like to experience a runner's high? Or how about enjoying half an hour working out with no one to interrupt your thoughts? Find your motivation and focus on that as you plan your regime.

Aim for **20 minutes of moderate exercise every day,** such as brisk walking or anything else that raises your heart rate, or **three 25-minute sessions of more vigorous exercise per week** – think jogging, skipping or playing an energetic sport. Include some activities that **strengthen muscle** too, such as sit-ups, squats or push-ups, carrying heavy bags or digging the garden.

Design a plan that fits with your commitments, and pick activities that are enjoyable and allow you to progress. Training with others will give you encouragement and a social boost, so a weekly class of a sport you've always wanted to try could be an option. Perhaps you also have a spare half hour where you can give a home workout a go? You could combine exercise with other things you need to do, such as walking to the shop and carrying your bags back. Adding small bursts of activity to your routine helps too. How about doing squats while you wait for the dinner to cook? You can also boost the intensity of almost any activity: you could run up the stairs or use extra energy for the housework.

Have fun coming up with creative ways to get active and remember that everyone starts somewhere. The human body is an amazing machine that adapts as you use it. That first workout might be a struggle, but once you've done it you're on your way. Don't feel a failure if you can't dash out the door and run 5 km on day one... no one can. Every effort you make to be active counts. Start your new regime with enthusiasm, and the progress you make as your body responds will be all the encouragement you need to keep going.

EMBRACE HEALTHY EATING

We often underestimate the importance of nutrition and the effect it has on our energy levels and mood: positive dietary changes are a powerful way to supercharge your reset journey. Remind yourself of how hard your body works to carry you through the day. The food we eat fuels our bodies, and whenever we eat or drink we have the opportunity to choose something beneficial. Eating healthily doesn't need to be boring or feel restrictive. There are plenty of ways to eat tasty, unprocessed meals, bursting with flavour and nutrients.

The first step is to understand how to make healthier choices. **Added sugar** can cause headaches, weight gain, low mood and inflammation, so replace sweet desserts with fruit-based dishes, such as baked apples with dates, and swap chocolate bars for a square or two of dark chocolate. When it's time for a snack, try avocados, nuts and seeds, or a small amount of yoghurt or cheese if you eat dairy, as these foods tend to have less **salt** and **saturated fat** than processed snacks. (Watch out for low-fat products that include added sugar to boost flavour too.) It's a good idea to limit your **alcohol** and **caffeine** intake too, as our bodies need to work hard to process these and they have a negative effect on mood and sleep.

Making swaps might be challenging at first, but consider instead the wonderful range of fruits and vegetables, nuts, seeds and pulses available to you. These are packed with essential nutrients – they're what our bodies are designed to digest – and by choosing to include more of these in your diet, you're providing your body with exactly what it needs.

Remember that healthy habits are formed gradually; you don't have to overhaul your diet overnight. You could start by swapping one snack per day to a healthier choice, or changing one meal across the week and seeing how you feel. Don't feel you have to cut out the things you love either. A lifestyle that involves enjoying treats in moderation is far more sustainable – and enjoyable – than one that means never eating cake again. You're not aiming for an all-or-nothing health streak; you're making a long-term commitment to a healthier path. Every choice is an opportunity, and every natural food you include will benefit your body.

Stay hydrated

Our bodies need water to perform at their best. Dehydration affects our mood and concentration levels, our quality of sleep and our bodies' ability to fight infection and regulate temperature. Most of us fall short when it comes to drinking enough water, so make a conscious effort to not just carry a water bottle with you, but to drink from it too!

You may know that we should drink around eight glasses of water a day... so challenge yourself to actually do this, refilling your glass every hour or so during the working day for example. You'll be amazed at the difference it makes: you'll feel energized and more alert. If water isn't your thing, you can drink herbal teas and include a smoothie for a vitamin boost, but avoid caffeinated drinks, which will dehydrate you, and stick to just one glass of fruit juice a day (as this can be high in sugar).

Take care
of your body.
It's the only place
you have to live.

Jim Rohn

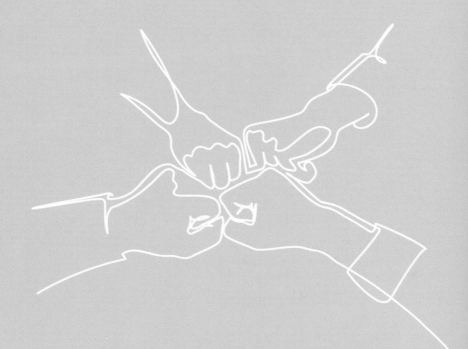

FIND
YOUR TRIBE.

People power

Humans are social creatures, and we've evolved to be part of a group, which is why positive interactions with other people matter to us and can provide such a boost to our mental health. When you're resetting your life, it's important to make interactions a priority. We'll look at different ways to build connections in Part Four, but some simple tips to try right away include:

- calling a friend while you're walking to work – or even better, meeting up with them

- smiling at people

- just saying hello – to the next person in line at the supermarket... the mail person... the next person you pass in the street...

- writing a letter to a friend

- getting to know someone new at work

- paying someone a compliment

- carrying out an act of kindness for a stranger

- inviting a neighbour in for coffee

Part Three:

WHERE DO I WANT TO BE?

You've taken stock and identified the things that matter to you most, now comes the exciting part – looking to the future and working out where you'd like your reset journey to take you. What are your ambitions? How can you fulfil your purpose? And what elements would you like to include in your happier, healthier and more meaningful life? This chapter includes inspiration, prompts and activities to help you answer these questions and set achievable goals.

BUILD A BUCKET LIST

Start by dreaming big and writing your bucket list – what are the things you've always wanted to do? What would you do now if you had the time and money? The sky's the limit when it comes to what you include, and there are no wrong answers, so use the ideas below to prompt you and see where your dreams would take you.

Places I'd like to go:

....

....

....

Sights I'd like to see:

....

....

....

Wildlife I'd like to encounter:

....

....

....

People I'd like to meet:

....

....

....

Skills I'd like to learn:

....

....

....

Crazy things I'd like to do:

....

....

....

Things my friends have done that I'd like to do:

....

....

....

Things I've wanted to do since I was a child:

....

....

....

LIFE'S A
JOURNEY –
FIND THE
WONDER IN
EVERY STEP.

WHAT WAS YOUR CHILDHOOD DREAM?

It can be revealing and rewarding to think a little more about your childhood dreams. These ambitions surfaced before we learned to care too much about other people's opinions, and they relate to the values and interests that have always mattered to us – they're drawn from a well of pure inspiration. Remind yourself of your childhood ambitions, and write about them in your journal or reminisce about them with a family member.

What was it about these aspirations that appealed to you so much? Can you find a way to honour them now you're an adult? Think creatively – if you always wanted to be an astronaut, for example, could you get a telescope and try stargazing, or plan a trip to see the Northern Lights? Rediscovering these early ambitions will help you tune in to the feeling of wonder you felt as a child about the world around you and your place in it.

IMAGINE YOUR IDYLL

Creative visualization is a simple but effective way for you to focus on where you want to be and how you would like to feel in the future. It can help you to set goals and achieve them too. To give it a try, find somewhere where you won't be disturbed, and sit quietly for a moment, focusing on your breathing.

Now picture yourself as you'd like to be – a happier and more fulfilled you – including as much detail as you like. How do you look? Where are you? Who is with you? And, most importantly, how do you feel? Meditate on the joy of being your future self and inhabit this for a while. Note down any interesting thoughts in your journal after you've finished.

You can repeat this meditation whenever you like, adding details or simply enjoying the experience, and using it to inspire you while you work toward achieving this happiness.

The future belongs
to those who believe
in the beauty of
their dreams.

Eleanor Roosevelt

A "WHY" MIND MAP

Numerous studies have shown that contributing to something we consider to be worthwhile is essential for our happiness, but even without the science to back it up many of us know that this makes sense as we will recognize it in our own lives. We're naturally enthusiastic about things we feel passionate about, which motivates us to achieve results and means we take pleasure in what we've done.

Look back at page 48 to remind yourself of your biggest motivation, then take a large sheet of blank paper and write it in a bubble at the centre of it. This is your purpose. Now consider all the ways in which you could achieve your purpose and record all your ideas. You can dot them around randomly or you might like to group ideas according to different areas of your life.

The important thing is to go for quantity over quality – fill the page with inspiration. Don't judge or edit your ideas; just let them flow and write everything down, no matter how crazy! If you're feeling creative, you can go one step further and make a mood board of your ideas with sketches or photos. You could also do this digitally, creating and seeking inspiration from pinboards online.

Once you're done, you can then use your mind map as inspiration when you're setting specific goals, making general decisions or choosing what to do with your free time.

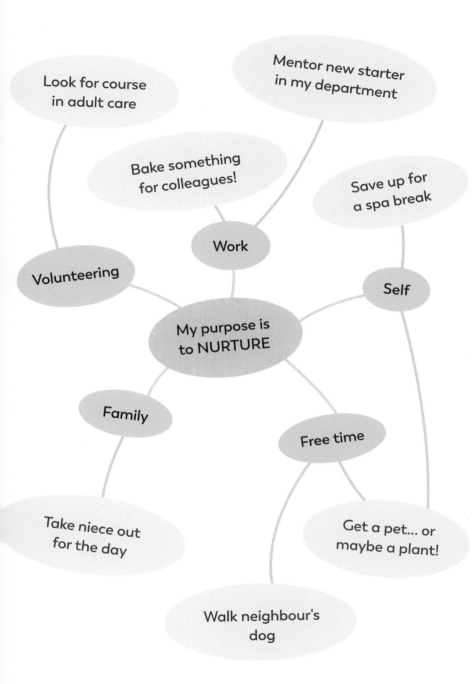

Look for course in adult care

Mentor new starter in my department

Bake something for colleagues!

Save up for a spa break

Work

Volunteering

Self

My purpose is to NURTURE

Family

Free time

Take niece out for the day

Get a pet... or maybe a plant!

Walk neighbour's dog

SET YOUR GOALS

Your reset journey needs direction, and goals will give you something to work toward. You may want just one goal, or you may like to consider all the areas you reviewed in Part One and identify one for each. They don't all need to be huge long-term projects. Simple goals count too!

If you're setting an ambitious goal, give some thought to how you'll achieve it. If it will take three years of hard study, for example, and you're not a keen student, it might not be the best choice for you. But pick something you'll enjoy working toward and you have an excellent chance of success. Remember that the goals you choose should be things that you want to achieve, not things that you think you ought to do or tasks you're taking on to impress others. It's important that you have a positive, healthy motivation behind your plans.

Use the table on the next page to get you thinking; fill the whole thing in or just focus on the areas that interest you. You can look back over the ideas you've mind-mapped so far to help, then – bearing in mind your strengths and interests – see if you can come up with a list of goals you'd like to achieve that inspire and excite you, and which deserve a place in your reset life.

LIFE AREA	MY GOAL IS...
Work	
Health and fitness	
Self-development	
Family	
Relationship	
Hobbies	
Self-care	
Home	
Ambitions	
Travel	
Goal from my bucket list	
Other dreams/ goals	

Setting work goals

For many of us, our job will take up a large proportion of our time – whether that's paid work, homemaking or any other cause we give our time to. It's worth giving some extra thought to this area as how you feel about it will have a huge impact on your happiness levels overall. If you feel stuck in a rut or unhappy in your current role, here are some ways to get inspiration and think about a change of direction:

1. Mind-map different ways to put your skills and talents to use.

2. Take an online careers questionnaire to discover potential new vocations.

3. Speak to people who have your dream job to get inspired (or to adjust your dreams!)

4. Volunteer in an area you're interested in to get a feel for whether it would work for you.

5. Subscribe to online forums or industry magazines to research an area of interest.

6. Chat to your friends about their dream jobs – and see what they could imagine you doing for a career.

7. Take an online course to develop your interest.

I will not
follow where the
path may lead;
instead I will
go where there
is no path and
leave a trail.

Muriel Strode

NURTURE YOURSELF AND YOU WILL GROW.

SET A SELF-DEVELOPMENT GOAL

When you picture your future self, do you consider *how* you would like to be, as well as where? Most of us imagine a calmer, happier version of ourselves – and resetting your life can help to bring that person into being – but what about other character traits? Would you like to be more confident or decisive? These are all qualities you can work on and develop with practice.

Setting self-development goals means making a positive commitment to learn from and improve your life experiences – they're not about setting out to correct a fault in your personality! Every single one of us can benefit from self-improvement and there's no shame in realizing, for example, that you could improve your listening skills or be a little more patient. So pick a goal, set yourself a self-development challenge and review your progress in a month or so.

The authentic you

Lots of us present a persona to the world that doesn't quite fit with who we are. It's often necessary for a role we play in life – we may need to be particularly accommodating with customers at work, for example – but it's important that we don't lose sight of our own thoughts, preferences and beliefs the rest of the time.

We've inherited the desire to belong from our ancient ancestors, who needed approval to survive, but today there's no need to downplay your individuality to fit in. Would your interactions be different if other people's opinions weren't a factor? What would you say if you spoke your mind? Remind yourself of your guiding principles (see page 46) and act in accordance with these, rather than the way you think others expect. We can never second-guess what others think of us and, more importantly, it doesn't matter! Be true to yourself and your beliefs instead.

To be yourself
in a world that is
constantly trying to
make you something
else is the greatest
accomplishment.

Ralph Waldo Emerson

Part Four:

HOW WILL I GET THERE?

You've taken stock, identified your priorities and thought about how you would like your reset life to look – now it's time to make it happen. This chapter is bursting with ideas to help you put your plans into action. You'll learn to use your time more productively, discover how to work toward your goals and find out how to keep up your enthusiasm and motivation. There's no pressure to tackle everything in this chapter at once – you can take things at your own pace – but you'll see results as soon as you get started with these simple, achievable tips.

Ready to reset?

It can be helpful to have a final declutter to prepare for your fresh start. Have a look at:

1. **Your schedule:** thin down your commitments, delegating or declining extra tasks, and streamlining chores to use your time efficiently (see page 90).

2. **Your relationships:** minimize contact with difficult people and prioritize good friends instead.

3. **Your home:** it's hard to make a fresh start when you've got a houseful of clutter – have a good sort--out, going through paperwork, unwanted gifts, and clothes that no longer fit.

4. **Your thoughts:** we all experience regrets and negative thought patterns, but we can learn to challenge these and embrace positive thinking. We'll look at how to do this in the following pages.

Remember: you don't need to tackle all this in one go, but declutter a little at a time and you'll feel better for the changes you make.

The ability to simplify
means to eliminate
the unnecessary so
that the necessary
may speak.

Hans Hofmann

KEEPING TIME

You've already taken a look at how you spend your week and have hopefully cut down on any commitments that didn't fit with your sense of purpose. However, there are other ways to tweak your schedule and free up some time to work toward your goals or pursue your hobbies.

Look for periods of **wasted time** during your week. Time spent waiting in traffic or checking social media, for example, adds up. Could you use it more productively: listening to a podcast, browsing for inspiration for your dream project or having short bursts of study instead? Alternatively, cut down on checking your social media and crack on with something else so that you gain an extra hour at the end of the day.

Find ways to **get your chores done more efficiently**. It's easier to clear up as you go, for example, rather than leaving everything to sort out at the end of the day. (If you see something that needs doing, and it takes less than 5 minutes, do it straightaway!) If you're going upstairs, downstairs, to the car, to the shops... what else can you take with you to save a trip later? And what about using the time while you're waiting for the washing to spin to lay out your clothes or pack your work bag for the day ahead?

For the chores you have to do every day, see if you can **put a positive spin on them,** listening to music while you clean the car, for example, or seeing the school run as a chance to laugh and connect with your children. You can also turn any chore into a mindful moment – by focusing on the details of what you're doing and your breathing as you do it – and use it as a peaceful pause in your daily routine.

And finally, if you really want to have some extra time to pursue your dream, **make it**. Getting up half an hour earlier than usual every day (or staying up half an hour later, if you're a night owl) will add up to three extra hours a week. Give it a try for a week or two – you never know, you might find that your sacred 30 minutes working on your dream is well worth losing a little sleep for.

EVERY DAY
IS A NEW
ADVENTURE!

Get organized

Getting organized will save you time and cut stress, so you'll feel calmer and happier every day. Devise a good routine for your workdays and make sure all the essentials – your keys, bag, work clothes, etc. – are easy to grab when you leave. Put up some extra hooks or shelves to store them if necessary. Anything that saves you from running around in a last-minute panic is a plus. Prepare ahead anything you need for the following day: if you want to fit some exercise in, for example, get your kit ready and leave it somewhere prominent!

Don't forget to plan ahead to include the fun things too: a half-hour break to listen to music when you get home or a coffee with your friend every Saturday morning is just as important as anything else on your to-do list. Make these a part of your weekly routine so that you don't miss out.

THAT FRESH-START FEELING

The feeling that you're starting something new is an exciting and inspiring one – remember the optimism we often feel at the start of a new year? You don't need to wait for the first of January to tune in to the power of a new beginning, though: try some of these ideas to bring a sense of adventure to the day ahead.

1. Wear something new or experiment with a different look.

2. Style your hair differently; try a new colour if you're feeling bold.

3. Start a new exercise programme or learn a new sport one step at a time.

4. Take a different route to work.

5. Smile or chat to someone you've never spoken to before.

6. Start a family tradition.

7. Buy a new notebook and use it for your latest project.

8. Learn something new – a party trick or a few words of a different language.

9. Choose a different option for lunch or cook a new dish for supper.

Make new connections

Meeting new people can be a very positive part of your reset process. It gives you a chance to make a fresh start – in line with the new values and priorities you've explored – and to introduce the new authentic you to others. Enjoy being this version of yourself and building new bonds. It can be particularly rewarding to meet people who share your interests and values. You can do this by volunteering for a cause that matters to you, or taking up a new hobby, doing a course, joining a book group or sports team, or finding a forum to join online.

Enjoy your encounters with *any* new acquaintances, though. There's always something to learn from others, and it's good to experience new opinions and open our minds to different points of view. Now you are confident in your own core values, these discussions should be interesting and enlightening rather than a cause for disagreement.

CHOOSE A NEW CHALLENGE

Studies have shown that challenging ourselves gives us a great feeling of accomplishment and boosts our well-being. Your chosen activity should be demanding, but fun and achievable. Here are some ideas to get you started:

PHYSICAL

- learn to do a headstand or handstand
- train to run a particular distance
- teach yourself to juggle... if that's too easy, try adding another ball!
- learn to do the splits or a kip-up
- perfect some football tricks

MENTAL

- memorize some poetry or lyrics to recite for friends
- become an expert at solving sudoku
- recite the alphabet backward
- show off with some flashy mental arithmetic
- solve a Rubik's cube
- learn a list of queens and kings, or presidents

OTHER

- tackle a TikTok challenge
- peel an orange in one piece
- learn some magic
- balance a drink can on its edge
- roll a coin between your fingers

DON'T SET
LIMITS;
SET GOALS.

CHALLENGE NEGATIVE THINKING

We're predisposed to use certain thinking styles that put a negative spin on our circumstances and can prevent us from seeing things as they really are. Take a look at the examples on the next page and see if any seem familiar. These aren't things you're "doing wrong" – many are reflex responses inherited from our ancestors – but with a little work you can learn to spot them and adjust your point of view to a more balanced one.

You can probably see from these examples that there are more realistic – and less upsetting – alternatives to the negative pictures we draw for ourselves. Often, just being aware that our thoughts can run away with us will remind us that we don't always see an accurate picture of a situation. Another useful way to counteract unhelpful thinking is to:

- **pause when you notice it**

- **take some calming breaths**

- **focus on a positive thought**

- **"reframe" your thinking before you take any action**

THINKING STYLE	WHAT IT MEANS	EXAMPLE
Catastrophizing	Immediately assuming that the worst-case scenario is going to happen	"I've missed the bus, now I'm going to be late for work and lose my job!"
Negativity bias	Focusing on a single negative aspect in an otherwise positive situation	You ignore praise from your colleagues for a well-delivered presentation and focus on a jokey remark from the office clown who didn't like your choice of shoes.
"All or nothing" thinking	If things aren't perfect, they're a complete disaster	"If I don't get one hundred per cent on my exam, I've failed."
Jumping to conclusions	Assuming you understand why something has happened or what will happen in the future	Someone checks their watch while talking to you and you "know" that they're bored in your company.
Over-generalizing	Seeing patterns based on a single event or drawing overly wide conclusions	"I was so nervous before making that speech at my friend's wedding... I'm terrible at public speaking."
Personalization	Blaming yourself for something that wasn't your responsibility	A friend sounds upset on the phone and cuts short your call – you're convinced you've done something to upset them.

The power of positivity

Practising positivity helps us to correct negative thinking and take a brighter, more optimistic attitude to life. If you've labelled yourself as a pessimist, that's no excuse! It's possible to change our style of thinking thanks to the neuroplasticity of our brains, which create new neural pathways when we start thinking in a different way. Train yourself to find the positives in tricky situations and try to use more positive language too. Rather than seeing a mishap as a "disaster" call it a "hitch", or relabel a "problem" as a "challenge".

Developing an attitude of gratitude can have further-reaching benefits too – studies show that optimists are more likely to embrace life's challenges, succeed and enjoy positive mental health. You'll find it easier to reframe tricky situations in the moment too, and will be well-practised at finding another focus when you're experiencing stress or panic.

BE GRATEFUL FOR THE DETAILS

Recording the high points of your day in a gratitude journal is a great way to focus on the positives (see page 42), but you can take this further by turning your reflections into an exercise in mindfulness. Pick the moment from your day that you're most grateful for and relax into the memory. Think about the details, engaging as many of your senses as you can while you recreate what happened. Finally, think about what it was you really valued about the experience – was it the connection you felt with another person or the world around you? Or a feeling of achievement when you completed a work project? Or the satisfaction of helping a stranger out? Make a note of this in your journal and look out for other opportunities to recreate that feeling in the future.

A fresh start is a
journey – a journey
that requires a plan.

Vivian Jokotade

Mini resets

Here are some ideas for speedy pick-me-ups to use whenever you need to boost your mood or energy levels.

- open a window – breathe in fresh air and focus on the birdsong

- yawn, stretch, then tense and release your muscles, starting at your feet and working upward

- cuddle or connect with someone – a friend or an animal companion

- do a quick set of jumping jacks, squats or push-ups

- sing aloud to a favourite track – dancing optional!

- go outside for a brisk walk

- think of – or watch – something that makes you laugh

LEAVING THE PAST BEHIND

We are all shaped by our past. The events that happened to us as children, our relationships with our parents and our past traumas can have an effect on the way we think, feel and behave. If today you find certain situations difficult to handle, can't understand why an innocent remark can trigger you to overreact, or experience feelings of anxiety or depression, it's likely that an unaddressed problem from the past is the root cause. Don't worry: you're experiencing a natural reaction to what has happened, and the good news is that it's possible to process these events and move forward. You may even find positives to take away from challenging situations.

If these "past ripples" are mild ones, you may well be able to work through them yourself. See if you notice a pattern occurring – what triggers your feelings? Take some time to think about what may have caused this reaction. When did you first feel this way? Journaling about your feelings or talking them through with a close friend can be a good way to start healing, as simply acknowledging why you feel the way you do is very powerful. Remember to treat yourself with compassion as you reflect on your situation – looking back on difficult times can trigger feelings that are as strong and immediate as they were when you first experienced them.

Releasing any pent-up emotion is key to healing, so be prepared for a few tears. Speaking your thoughts aloud can be a good way of venting your feelings, and writing them down is always beneficial. If you feel that someone has treated you badly in the past you could write a letter to the person in question. You don't need to send it, of course – simply expressing your feelings will help.

For deeper issues, seeing a counsellor can have really beneficial results. They'll provide a non-judgemental ear and will be able to advise you on practical things to do to move on. Talk to your medical professional or check online to see what options are available. (It may be worth paying for a couple of consultations if you can afford it, to set you off on the road to healing.)

With time, try to see what positives you can take away from your situation – apart from the fact that you've gone through a difficult time and come out the other side, which is pretty amazing in itself. What have you learned about yourself? You've probably discovered that you're stronger than you thought you were. You may have learned how to reach out to others for support and built up better relationships with those around you. Or perhaps you've learned to appreciate life more. You'll be able to carry these strengths forward with you, and leave the more painful aspects of your experience behind.

PURSUE YOUR PURPOSE, FOLLOW YOUR PATH.

Ground yourself

Grounding involves renewing your connection with the earth beneath you and it's a perfect antidote when your feelings are running out of control.

1. Sit comfortably – outside if possible – close your eyes and focus on the sounds around you.

2. Inhale to a count of four, hold your breath and then exhale for six in turn.

3. Focus on the parts of your body that are in contact with the ground and picture warm healing energy flowing up into these areas from the earth beneath you.

4. Feel this energy spreading through your body as you continue to breathe slowly.

5. Exhale any tension as you breathe out, and inhale warm healing energy to replace it.

6. Finish by gently opening your eyes, shaking out your body and returning to your day feeling revitalized.

Once you've practised this, you'll be able to tap into this grounded feeling whenever you need – even if you can't make it to your favourite grounding spot.

RESET YOUR BODY CLOCK

Getting a good sleep routine in place will regulate your body clock, which controls everything from your mood to your energy levels. It's one of the most effective resets you can make.

If you can take some time out from your commitments, it's interesting to spend a few days waking without the use of an alarm and getting up when you feel rested, eating simple meals when you feel hungry and then napping and sleeping when your body feels ready to do so. This will give you an idea of when you feel naturally more alert or energetic so that you can plan activities – such as study or exercise – for the times that suit you best.

Ideally, we would wake with the daylight, have a short nap mid-afternoon (when our energy levels need a boost) and wind down to sleep at the same time every night. This isn't practical for everyone, but you should be able to tweak your routine to benefit your body clock. Try to:

1. Get up and go to bed at a similar time every day.

2. Soak in some bright natural light around 10 minutes after waking.

3. Eat your meals at regular times.

4. Avoid caffeine in the last 5 hours before you sleep.

5. Avoid eating and exercising in the last couple of hours before bed.

6. Avoid using devices with screens in the last hour or so.

This will help your body clock to stabilize and wind down ready for a restorative night's sleep. Many people find that restricting the time they eat during the day – to a 10- or 12-hour window – benefits their metabolism too. If you work shifts or have problems with your sleep cycle, light therapy – using a light box at the same time every day – may help to reset your body's rhythms and improve your sleep.

It's also rewarding to carry out a relaxing bedtime ritual every evening. Yours could include:

1. Preparing your things for the next day while you run a warm bath.

2. Any daily beauty/pamper treatments.

3. A warm caffeine-free drink.

4. Jotting down any worries and setting them aside to think about the following day.

5. Reading or listening to a podcast.

6. Journaling or thinking through the highlights of your day.

7. Meditating or stretches.

A REBOOT-YOUR-DAY RITUAL

Every morning is a new beginning, but this *doesn't* mean you have to leap out of bed and start dashing through your to-do list. In fact, starting the day with a moment of calm reflection is a powerful way to press "reboot". It will leave you feeling grounded and better prepared to face the day's challenges.

Set your alarm early enough to give you 15 minutes to ease into the day before you start your morning routine. If your current alarm leaves your heart racing, pick a melody that starts softly and gradually gets louder, or choose a clock that wakes you with a gentle glow of light (with sound as a backup), as this is a more natural, gradual way to wake up.

As you wake, spend a few moments simply "being" and observing your thoughts. Your brain will have been busy while you sleep and might offer up ideas or inspiration, or you may be able to remember the tail end of an intriguing dream. (Keep your journal by your bed to note down anything interesting to think about later.) Notice your breathing – deep and slow – and imagine that you're inhaling calm positive energy and exhaling any tension about the day ahead. Gently engage with your senses, focusing on any sounds you can hear, the patterns of light coming through your curtains or the warmth of your bed covers.

If you have time, you could spend a few minutes journaling before you get up, reminding yourself of why you're brilliant (see page 27) or thinking about yesterday's moment of gratitude and carrying that joy forward into your morning.

If you'd like to set a goal for your day, do so, but don't overload your waking moments with "shoulds" and "must-dos". A more general goal is a nice idea: "Today I will look for the positives" or "I will live in the moment, embrace each challenge and know that I am enough". Or how about repeating this thought to finish your morning reboot:

It's the start of
a new day –
and anything
is possible!

GO FOR YOUR GOALS

Take a look back at page 79 and the goals you set for some of the different areas of your life. Which goal would you like to go for first? Have you got a plan in mind to help you achieve it? Breaking any task down into manageable steps is the best way to get it done, so make a list of the things you need to do to achieve your outcome, tune in to your inspiration and enthusiasm and take the first step as soon as possible.

You're much more likely to succeed if you can measure your progress as you go, so celebrate the wins as you take each step toward your dream. Indulge in a treat or share your story with others as you tick off each stage of the process. You may even find a challenge buddy who can share your journey and encourage you along the way.

Motivation is the powerful force that will keep you on track as you work toward your goals. While inspiration is the driving internal force that gives us direction, motivation is all about external prompts that keep us moving. We achieve so much more when we feel motivated, buzzing with the energy to get things done, but after that initial burst of enthusiasm we may find ourselves flagging, especially if the goal we've chosen is a tricky one to achieve. Stay motivated by:

- reminding yourself of why you want to achieve your goal

- picking an image or power word to sum up your motivation and focusing on that

- scheduling in regular times to work on your goal

- putting in just 15 minutes' effort on the days when you feel tired or unmotivated – once you get started you might feel inspired to do more

- sharing the journey with a friend or mentor

- being flexible – don't be afraid to change direction once you start

If you find that you "fail" or come to a bit of an impasse, consider why this has happened. What needs to change for you to succeed? Take a little time out to think about how you'd like to move forward, adjust your goal and then get going again.

PUT AN END TO PROCRASTINATION

Procrastination can hijack our plans and prevent us from moving on toward better things. It's easy to feel frustrated or unsettled with a raft of uncompleted tasks or unmade decisions hanging over you. Make an effort to notice when you procrastinate and consider what's holding you back. Do you shy away from decisions through lack of confidence? Or do you tell yourself you don't have time to carry out your task? None of these are good reasons to press pause on your plans. To move forward in life, take a step, even if it's a small one.

If you're dreading doing something, take the bull by the horns and get it out of the way – you'll feel so much better for taking action. Or perhaps subconsciously you're procrastinating because you don't want to move a task forward? This is important to acknowledge too.

Don't let anyone tell you what you can or cannot do, or cannot achieve. Just don't allow it.

Emma Watson

MORE MIND RESETS

Here are a few more self-development ideas to consider when you're resetting yourself. Remember, these are not things you're currently getting "wrong" – they are perfectly normal mental habits – but if you acknowledge them and refocus, life can become much more positive.

Make helpful comparisons

It's in our nature to compare ourselves to others, but it's not a helpful or even realistic exercise. Remember that everyone is different, and everyone has off days. When you find yourself comparing your lot with someone else's, find a positive outcome by showing them compassion or empathy, for example, or using their success to motivate yourself.

Don't take it personally

It's natural to feel hurt if someone treats you poorly, but learning not to take these slights personally makes life much easier. The only time you should feel upset about bad behaviour is if you've carried it out; if someone else has behaved badly, that's their issue. Don't take these incidents to heart – focus on pleasant and positive interactions with good friends instead.

Don't dwell on the past or stress about the future

Past regrets and future worries have such a negative impact on the present day. Mindfulness exercises, such as grounding yourself or focusing on your breathing, are a great antidote to this as they bring your attention to the present moment. Try to practise these every day.

If you find yourself dwelling on the past, release any regrets or bitterness (see page 104) if possible and make a conscious effort to focus on a present-day blessing instead. If worries about the future are pressing in, set aside 5 minutes to worry, and then continue with your day. If your worry is a genuine issue, work out what you can do to change things, or where you can get advice, then take action.

Get rid of guilt

It's easy to think we could have done things differently given hindsight, but guilt weighs you down and doesn't change the past. Get perspective on your situation, seeing it from another point of view if possible. You did the best you could in the circumstances so forgive yourself... or offer an apology and make amends if you genuinely feel you were in the wrong.

Retune your senses

Resetting your life is all about simplification – stripping away the "stuff" that clutters our thoughts and clogs our days, so that we can concentrate on the things that matter and bring us pleasure. Find and focus on some simple pleasures, absorbing and enjoying their details, and, as your activity takes on a mindful element, you'll not only feel happier but calmer too.

Pick something to appeal to one of your senses: an awe-inspiring or beautiful image to look at; a wonderful aroma; your favourite food to taste; a mood-boosting piece of music or the relaxing sounds of nature; a soft blanket to touch or some bubble wrap to pop! Focus on the details of your chosen item or experience, and enjoy tuning in to your senses and giving them a treat. This simple activity is a wonderful way to slow down the pace and tune in to the present moment.

Find your way

If you're feeling lost mentally, you may be able to set yourself on a surer path. Scientists have identified a link between a person's navigational skills and their sense of purpose. Activities that develop the hippocampus region of the brain – such as orienteering and map-reading – can help us to regain our sense of direction, both figuratively and literally. (And since they're activities that get us outside, they're doubly beneficial.)

Get hold of a map for your local area, or look one up on an app, and explore footpaths and features near you. Plan out a route beforehand and look out for the landmarks on your map. You could also try finding a new route through town and following it from memory, or creating your own map of the area and marking on your favourite places.

RELATIONSHIP RESETS

It's easy to take our close relationships for granted when our lives are full of commitments and activities, but it's important to prioritize time to maintain and enjoy our links with our loved ones. Sometimes, though, our relationships go through more challenging stages, and you may need to take action so that you can move forward on more positive footing.

If you've neglected time with your partner or family, it is easy to reboot your relationship with small thoughtful gestures and kind words, and by planning some simple but precious moments together. You could cook a special meal, picnic in your lunch hour or take an evening walk. Learning new skills together, mixing with different groups of people or going to places you've never visited before are also good ways to inject some new energy into your relationship and remind you of what you love about one another.

If you feel that past issues are putting pressure on a relationship, think about how you might clear the air and move on, either by talking things through or writing a letter for your loved one to read and consider in their own time. Both of you should have an opportunity to express how you feel, and should listen to and acknowledge the other person's feelings. Be prepared to apologize for your own shortcomings and forgive your loved one if you're willing and able to move on. If the same little issues bug you about one another time and again, try to come up with ways to accommodate these together.

If you feel that you have been seriously wronged, however, or that your relationship is in a very negative state, only you can decide whether it's something you can and should recover from. Either way, you must find a way forward, because past negativity can cast a real shadow over the present. Don't be afraid to ask for help from a counsellor or advice from a trusted friend.

It can be useful to have some relationship "yardsticks" in mind as you move forward to a more positive place. Think about what is and isn't acceptable behaviour in a relationship or friendship. Everyone will have different ideas about this, but talking it through with others can help you to consider and establish some relationship rules to guide you in the future.

NEW OPPORTUNITIES

Once you've streamlined your schedule it's important to use your precious remaining free time wisely and to include activities that are in line with your values, or that bring you happiness in other ways. First and foremost, ensure that you have some time to yourself built into your schedule every day, and hopefully you've also found a fun way to fit in some exercise too. With these basics in place, consider how you can add some new activities to your week that will fit your sense of purpose.

Volunteering

Whatever your skill set and whichever causes you believe in, you're sure to be able to find a volunteering opportunity to suit you. Helping others gives us a great sense of satisfaction, brings us into contact with like-minded people and has been shown to improve our mental health – in addition to the benefits we bring to others through our good works. Do some research to find local organizations who need your skills, or consider volunteering in a more informal way: helping an elderly neighbour with chores, litter-picking at a beauty spot or listening to children read at your local school. Volunteering can also be a good way to explore a different career you might like to pursue.

Hobbies

Our hobbies are one of the first things we abandon when life fills up with commitments and chores, so make sure that your new reset schedule includes time for you to pursue them again. If your hobby involves any equipment, make sure that it's stored somewhere easily accessible, and set aside a dedicated space for your pastime if you can – a sewing corner or space in the garage for your bike and tools. Then schedule in at least one session a week.

If you've always wanted to try something new, now's the time to give it a go, and signing up to a beginners' course is a great start. You'll be learning alongside people who share your interest and are also new starters, so everyone will be in the same boat. As well as being great fun, building your confidence and giving you the chance to meet new people, research has shown that learning new skills is beneficial for our mental health and can even boost our brainpower too. (One study revealed that language learners developed the creative part of their brain as well as the part that's responsible for language.)

RESET YOUR FINANCES

Your finances might not be your favourite topic, but they're an important one, and it's well worth revisiting how you're spending your money as part of your reset process. Set aside a couple of hours to go through your expenses and you'll reap the rewards of your financial review, especially if your new plans need some money behind them.

Take a look at all your regular outgoings and cut out anything you don't need or that doesn't fit with your new, reset purpose. Underused subscriptions or memberships can be a waste – remember you can exercise for free rather than going to the gym, and buy magazines as and when you have time to read them.

Plan your weekly food shop to benefit from multibuys and seasonal bargains, as this helps you to avoid food waste and costly top-up shops throughout the week. Cooking double quantities of food and freezing them is a great time- and money-saver too.

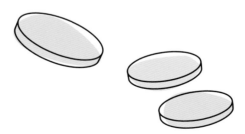

Shop around for new deals for all your basic utilities. Price comparison sites take all the stress out of shopping for new providers and will handle the switch-over process too, so this is well worth doing. Never accept a renewal quote for insurance without spending 10 minutes shopping for competitive quotes and ringing your service provider for their best counter-offer. You can save hundreds of pounds or dollars this way.

If you have debts hanging over you, tackle them – you need to clear past debts before you can start saving, and there's plenty of free and impartial advice available on how to do this online. Creditors may consider freezing your interest rate if you contact them and explain your repayment plans.

Try a 30-day financial reboot: set aside a budget for food, travel and utilities for the month and write this down, then challenge yourself to spend nothing else for the next 30 days. (Your frugal month might even free up some time for you to indulge in some more simple pleasures and self-care.) Use this time to think about what is really essential to you financially – and whether these things fit with your purpose and new plans – before you add your luxury spends back in at the end of the month.

YOU DON'T NEED
TO HAVE A PLAN
FOR EVERY STAGE
OF YOUR JOURNEY.
JUST TAKE THE
FIRST STEP.

Recipe for a reset

Here's a reminder of what to aim for...

1. A job or role that uses your skills and fits your sense of purpose.

2. Time to reflect and process your feelings.

3. Goals to help you achieve your dreams or pursue new adventures.

4. Self-development ideas.

5. An enjoyable exercise routine.

6. A healthy and nutritious diet, plus enough hydration.

7. A regular routine for sleep and meals.

8. Time to do the things you love.

9. Altruistic acts – volunteering or random acts of kindness.

10. Moments and methods for relaxation.

11. Time spent interacting with positive people.

If any of these things are missing from your life at the moment, try to add them to your routine in some way, however small. A cheerful hello to your delivery person is an act of kindness and may be an interaction, if you chat. Ten minutes of sit-ups and star jumps while you watch Netflix counts as exercise, plus you're doing something you love!

Part Five:

WHAT DOES MY SUPPORT SYSTEM LOOK LIKE?

There's plenty of help and support out there for you as you reset your life and move on to enjoy it, so don't feel that you're alone on your journey. It's good to have people on side to celebrate your successes with, and if you're facing a difficult week, struggling to move forward or just feeling a bit low, knowing who to chat to for some advice or a happiness boost can make all the difference.

In this chapter we look at how to identify your allies and build a solid support network to help you tackle whatever challenges life throws at you. And don't forget that there are lots of ways you can support yourself too – you'll find ideas for this scattered throughout the chapter.

Friends and family

Our family and friends should be an obvious first port of call when we need help, but life can be complicated, and this is a call we don't always make. If you shy away from "bothering" your loved ones, you're missing out on valuable support. How would you react if *they* had a problem? Of course, you'd want to help – and no doubt your loved ones would like to support you too.

Many of us find asking for help difficult, but having someone to share your concerns with is essential for positive mental health, so get together a list of your supportive friends and family members as a reminder of who to turn to when you need a boost. It doesn't have to be the same person every time, and they don't need to offer solutions. Often, simply listening is enough... and of course this is something you can do for your loved ones in return.

Anything is possible when you have the right people there to support you.

Misty Copeland

A GOOD FRIEND
DOUBLES YOUR
JOY AND HALVES
YOUR SORROW.

Pick a partner

You'll enjoy your reset journey even more if you have a good travelling companion by your side. If you're setting yourself a challenging goal, buddy up with a friend to encourage you and help you stay on track. If your challenge buddy has their own project in mind, that's even better – you can support one another and share your enthusiasm as you work toward your goals.

Setting up a regular meet – whether it's a real-world get-together or an online chat – is a great idea. By scheduling in time to discuss your plans, you're prioritizing your goals. You'll also want to have something to report back to your friend, so you'll stay motivated – and you could even set each other a task to complete before you next meet up. If there are a few of you, set up a dedicated chat group to encourage one another throughout the week.

EXPLORE ONLINE OPTIONS

There's a wealth of information and support available to you online, whatever challenge you're facing, so spend a little time researching some positive websites to bookmark and supportive groups to join. If you're currently living with anxiety, depression or other mental health issues – and one in four of us will experience this at some point in our lives – Mind and Young Minds in the UK, and Mental Health America and the National Alliance on Mental Illness (NAMI) are brilliant resources. Mind also offers peer support via Side by Side, their online community.

If you have a more specific challenge, search online for a forum dedicated to your issue. Knowing that other people understand exactly how you feel is a huge comfort and you will benefit from each other's wisdom and coping strategies. Check online too, for details of any support groups that meet near you.

You'll also find lots of support online if you're setting yourself a challenge, learning a new skill, pursuing a hobby or researching a new career. Whatever your area of interest, there will be forums and groups to join on your favourite social media platforms. Blogging or vlogging about your goal quest can be a great way of sharing and celebrating your progress with friends, or others who share your interest, and their support can help to keep you motivated too.

Make sure that your relationship with social media is a positive one, though. There's little point in checking in with your support group for a mood boost if you're also scrolling through pictures of perfection on Instagram and making unhelpful comparisons or looking at photos of your ex! Block any unpleasant or upsetting contacts, leave any groups where people fill the comments with negativity, and delete any apps that leave you feeling low or inadequate. Now fill your phone with positivity instead: sign up for an inspirational thought for the day; subscribe to a daily nature photo or science fact to experience awe and appreciation for the world around you; make encouraging, kind comments about other people's achievements; or post jokes or silly stories to share some laughter with your friends.

PROFESSIONAL HELP AND SUPPORT

If you're struggling with your mental health or finding it hard to move on from a difficult situation, reach out to healthcare professionals for some well-deserved support. There's no shame in asking for help, attending therapy or taking medication – these are brave and positive steps toward self-healing. Doctors and therapists are trained to support you, and talking to them could turn your life around.

Start with the mental health charities mentioned on page 134 and a call to your doctor, who will be able to advise you on the types of support available. Don't be afraid to try different methods if the first option isn't the best fit: look for professional recommendations online. Attending a support group is another excellent choice. In the UK you can visit hubofhope.co.uk to find support groups in your area, while mhanational.org can help in the US and headtohealth.gov.au is a great resource in Australia.

YOU DON'T
NEED FIXING – YOU
AREN'T BROKEN – JUST
UNDERSTAND AND
ACCEPT YOURSELF, AND
MOVE ON WITH LOVE.

Find a mentor

If you're pursuing a career goal, finding a mentor to advise you is an excellent move. You're looking for someone with plenty of experience in your area of interest – someone who has walked the path you're hoping to tread already. It's possible that you have a colleague or friend who has advised you before, and you could gradually develop this relationship into a mentor–mentee scenario, or perhaps you could approach a former boss or teacher to see if they can spare some time to share their wisdom.

Once you've found a mentor, show your appreciation for their help and make the most of the time they give you. In return you'll receive guidance, enjoy the benefit of their experience and get a new perspective on your situation. Mentoring can work in other areas of your life too: think of the worldly-wise people you know and respect, and see if you can build a mutually beneficial connection with them.

Be yourself, the world will adjust.

Manabi Bandyopadhyay

START A NEW RELATIONSHIP WITH YOURSELF

The most important new relationship in your reset journey is the one you build with yourself. Think about why you love your best friend. You love them flaws and all, not because they look perfect or got straight "A"s in their exams. It's our quirks that make us human and relatable... so find these qualities in yourself and fall in love with them. See yourself as your best friends do and start a relationship with yourself on those terms. Remind yourself of your achievements, focus on your good deeds, do kind things and believe in yourself.

Turn your awareness to your self-talk: whenever you take a negative tone toward yourself, pause and imagine that the person you're judging so harshly is someone you love. Picture yourself hugging them and extending words of comfort... then direct those warm feelings toward yourself, because you deserve them.

A loving-kindness meditation

This gentle meditation helps you to experience a renewed feeling of love toward yourself and others.

1. Find a peaceful place to meditate and sit comfortably. Close your eyes and focus on your breathing as you settle into stillness.

2. Imagine a feeling of deep and pure love – thinking of a loved one may help here. Feel it in your heart and picture it as a glowing ball of coloured light sending warmth throughout your body. Bask in this feeling of love and acceptance.

3. Think of your loved ones and send loving energy out to them: you might picture the ball of light expanding to envelop them.

4. Spread the loving-kindness further to your acquaintances, and finally anyone with whom you've had a disagreement.

5. Finish your meditation by extending thoughts of loving-kindness to the world around you, up into the heavens and down into the earth beneath your feet.

NURTURE NATURAL CONNECTIONS

Our fellow humans provide us with a strong support network, but it's rewarding to make connections with other living creatures too. Interacting with nature boosts our health, and there are plenty of ways to strengthen this link. Taking mindful walks and noticing the details of your surroundings is a good start. Visit a natural space regularly and you'll get to know its inhabitants – cheeky sparrows singing out their territorial claims or rabbits darting by at dusk... There's a constancy to these natural places that's so comforting to return to.

If you have animal companions in your life, spend quality time with them: enjoy their affection and nurture them in return. You can feed and watch wildlife that visits your garden or green space too. Your greatest support network is our planet's ecosystem, so connect with it regularly.

Spiritual support

If you haven't set aside time to explore your spirituality, it's a nice idea to give this some thought as you carry out your reset. Perhaps it's something you considered while you were thinking about the things that matter most to you, or perhaps it's an area you've never really explored. Browse the Mind, Body and Spirit section of a bookshop or search online to find an area of interest and read an inspirational book to start your spiritual journey.

If you have found your spiritual pathway or already belong to a religious community, you will know the support and comfort this can offer. Don't forget to access this and make time for your spiritual practice in your reset schedule. Meditating, practising yoga or listening to podcasts or talks are all good ways of developing your spirituality.

To get lost is to learn the way.

Swahili proverb

listen to your body

To support yourself, it's important to tune in to how you're feeling. Journaling and taking time out to process your thoughts are excellent ways to do this, but you can spot physical signs too. Try a body-scan meditation, where you spend a few minutes sitting quietly and focusing on different parts of your body in turn to identify any areas of tension or discomfort. If you're feeling stressed, for example, you may find that your shoulders are hunched, your jaw is clenched or your hands are curled into fists. Learn to recognize these signs and to release the tension when you spot it. If you're anxious you might feel discomfort in your stomach; panic might lead you to feel breathless; and headaches can be another sign of stress. Tune in to the signs that your body is giving you and take action when you notice them.

Trust your instincts

Just as your body gives you physical clues about your well-being, your subconscious can flag up your true feelings through instinctive thoughts. Learning to tune in to – and trust – your instincts can be very valuable and save you time overthinking things too... This doesn't mean that you should make major decisions on the spur of the moment, without proper thought, but do take notice of that first flash of a reaction, the way you feel in the pit of your stomach when you think about something. It's a gut reaction that shows your true feelings.

An easy way to tune in to this is to toss a coin when you're stuck with a decision. Note how you feel when you see the result and you'll have your answer – you'll soon realize whether you really wanted heads rather than tails, for example. Go with your gut and pick that option instead.

TRUST YOUR INTUITION; IT'S A MESSAGE FROM YOUR SOUL.

Swap failure for success

Become your own cheerleader by changing your attitude toward "failure" and finding new ways to measure success. Rather than berating yourself if you get something wrong, resolve to laugh about mishaps and learn from mistakes. It's unrealistic to expect to do everything perfectly, though this is the goal we often set ourselves. Instead, promise yourself you'll do your best and learn from the experience, whatever happens.

Remember that success is not measured by your earnings, qualifications or a perfect track record. If you've lived a day to the full and done something you enjoyed or that mattered to you, if you had moments when you felt truly alive and happy, or if you found time to offer kindness or service to someone else, your day has been a great success. Celebrate it! You should be very proud.

Failure is an
important part
of your growth
and developing
resilience. Don't
be afraid to fail.

Michelle Obama

WHAT TO DO WHEN THINGS GO WRONG

Even a reset life has its blips: moments when we feel we can't cope, or times when we feel stressed or triggered to react in ways we thought we'd left behind. Don't be hard on yourself when this happens. The good news is that, if you've learned a few new self-care techniques, you'll be in a much better position to cope.

Have a panic plan in place

If you suffer from anxiety attacks, knowing how to manage them will make an episode easier to deal with. When you recognize the signs, don't try to fight what's happening, but do try to find somewhere less stressful to wait things out. Sit down if possible, close your eyes and focus on breathing while making an "o" shape with your mouth. Remember that a longer out-breath will trigger a calming reaction in your nervous system, so focus on this. Having a panic buddy you can phone to talk to as you recover can be a big help too.

Emergency contacts

Think about who you could reach out to if you hit a rocky patch and put together a list of contacts to call, so that you won't need to spend time dithering or looking up numbers in the future. Your contact list could be a combination of trusted friends and support group numbers, and you could make it quite specific, detailing who to call in different types of situations. You may have one friend who is full of empathy and understanding, while another is straight-talking and will give you an honest opinion... no matter what!

Dealing with depression

In those moments when depression has the upper hand it can be very difficult to do anything constructive at all. Again, having a plan in place can help: you'll know what's most effective for you. Prepare everything you need ahead of time for some simple self-care activities. Getting outside, trying to focus on the positives, spending time with understanding, undemanding loved ones, or helping someone else with a task can all be effective coping strategies too. If the fog doesn't lift and you find that your change of spirits is affecting your day-to-day life long term, please reach out for help (see page 134). It is waiting for you and you deserve happiness.

MY SUPPORT RESOURCES

Use this page to make a note of the people and resources you can reach out to when you need a little support.

The best people I can call for advice are:

....

....

The best listener I can call is:

....

....

My panic buddy is:

....

....

The person who always cheers me up is:

....

....

Support groups to call in an emergency and their phone numbers are:

....

....

Useful websites to visit:

....

....

My favourite inspirational quotes:

....

....

The heroes who will inspire me when times are tough:

....

....

The TV shows to watch to cheer myself up:

....

....

The songs that comfort me:

....

....

Activities that calm me and help me to de-stress:

....

....

Things to have in my cheer-me-up pamper kit:

The best things I can do when I'm low:

Reset reminder

Keeping your reset on track is an ongoing process. It's important to regularly check in with yourself to make sure that your day-to-day life hasn't become diluted with distractions, and that you're still happy with your goals. Make reflection a habit, a small part of your daily routine, and you'll notice if things are going a little off course. Remember, you can reapply the reset process to your life at any time. Just:

- stop to check in with yourself

- reflect on what is and isn't working

- remind yourself of your priorities

- refocus on the things that matter

- reset yourself to pursue positive and purposeful activities

REST, REFLECT, RESTORE, RESET.

CONCLUSION

You've reached the end of the book – but your reset life is just beginning. Hopefully you've found plenty to inspire and encourage you to make some changes, and perhaps you're already enjoying the benefits of them! Remember that small changes really do add up and can tip the balance into making your days more fulfilling and joyful. Once you see the positive results of tweaking one area of your life, you'll feel open to other adjustments and new experiences. Most importantly, though, you'll be taking control of your time, your decisions and your journey ahead... and it's bound to be an exciting one. Perhaps you're already embarking on a bigger adventure and taking steps toward a career change or making a fresh start in another area of your life. If so, that's brilliant!

Take things at your own pace and remember that you can always return to these pages for guidance as you move forward, or to remind yourself of the reflections and thoughts you've jotted down. In fact, looking back on the fill-in sections after a little time has passed can be very rewarding – you'll notice the progress you've made since you started, and might come up with some new ideas to try or some fresh goals to aim for.

Wherever your reset path takes you, have fun and have confidence! If you let your talents shine, honour the things that matter to you, and move forward with the people you care about at your side, you can be sure that you're heading in the right direction.

Notes

....

....

....

....

....

....

....

....

....

....

....

....

....

....

....

....

....

....

Have you enjoyed this book?
If so, why not write a review on your favourite website?

If you're interested in finding out more about our books, find us on Facebook at **Summersdale Publishers**, on Twitter at **@Summersdale** and on Instagram at **@summersdalebooks** and get in touch. We'd love to hear from you!

Thanks very much for buying this Summersdale book.

www.summersdale.com